TO OWN A DONKEY

Jenifer Simpson

TO OWN A DONKEY

Angus & Robertson Publishers

ANGUS & ROBERTSON PUBLISHERS

Unit 4, Eden Park, 31 Waterloo Road,
North Ryde, NSW, Australia 2113
and
16 Golden Square, London W1R 4BN, United Kingdom

First published in Australia by Angus & Robertson Publishers in 1985
First published in the United Kingdom by Angus & Robertson (UK) Ltd in 1985

Copyright © Jenifer Simpson 1985

National Library of Australia
Cataloguing-in-publication data.
Simpson, Jenifer.
  To own a donkey.
  ISBN 0 207 15059 1.
  1. Donkeys — Juvenile literature. I. Title.
636.1′8

Design by Alison Windmill

Typeset in 11pt Century by Setrite Typesetters
Printed in Hong Kong

Acknowledgements

My thanks to Shona McDiarmid whose picture appears frequently in these pages. Without her cheerful support and refreshing enthusiasm, this book would have remained a dream.

Sincere thanks to the many members of the Queensland Branch of the Australian Donkey Breed Society who have helped. Their cooperation has been invaluable.

Above all, thanks to my donkeys for their patience, humour and wisdom. I hope they enjoyed it all as much as I did.

Jenifer Simpson
Teatree Donkey Stud,
Booloumba Creek,
Maleny, Queensland.

During the last ten years or so, the donkey has made a comeback and is now quite a common sight in the countryside. These donkeys are grazing as the morning mist starts to clear from Queensland's beautiful Conondale Range.

Contents

Donkeys seem to have a natural sympathy and affection for humans. They have infinite patience and are always ready to listen to our problems and share a joke. Yoyo appears to be listening, but he is thinking about grabbing a pigtail — just for fun!

Foreword

IN 1972, as Honorary Secretary of the newly formed Australian and New Zealand Donkey Breed Society, I found I was answering hundreds of letters from would-be donkey owners. They could have been divided into two categories: those who knew the donkey and those who had no personal knowledge of the "long-eared charmer".

People already aware of the mystique, history, legends and individual appeal of the animals wanted to know where to buy them and how to care for them, and glean any additional information they could obtain. The other category of inquirers always asked somewhere in the letter: "What do you *do* with donkeys?" Jenifer's book should appeal to both the initiated and uninitiated.

With more intelligence than a horse, but retaining a degree of independence similar to that found in the cat, donkeys continue to charm and intrigue those who know them. Anyone unable to understand their fascination may find some clues in this book. Above all other reasons for owning a donkey, I would have to agree that donkeys are for fun.

Jenifer Simpson, an industrial chemist who spent many years living on a yacht and exploring the tropical islands of the world, has settled in Maleny, Queensland, with her husband, Simon. There they practise a form of self-sufficiency liable to make any gourmet envious.

My first contact with Jenifer was when she began to contribute to the *Donkey Digest*, the magazine of the Australian Donkey Breed Society. Before long Jenifer became a regular contributor of enthusiastic, well-researched and informative articles. Jenifer breeds Australian donkeys and specialises in those under ten hands high.

I was not surprised when I heard she had embarked with her usual unlimited energy, boundless enthusiasm and attention to detail, on the project of preparing this book for publication.

To Own a Donkey covers most aspects of donkey ownership, from the delight of just watching them and the responsibilities entailed in ensuring correct care and management, to their training and the multitude of useful things they can do.

I look forward to the next 2000 years of the relationship between man and donkey.

Denice Moorhouse,
Editor,
Donkey Digest,
Magazine of the Australian
Donkey Breed Society.

Aged three minutes, Gypsy tries to take her first steps. Her legs are wobbly and she is not well-coordinated, so she falls over a few times. Incredibly, she soon gets her balance and legs under control.

Esmeralda, the mother, is very attentive and protective. She nudges the foal with her nose to encourage its efforts to rise and then pushes it in the direction of her udder.

Aged ten minutes, the foal takes its first nourishment.

A day after her birth, Gypsy's ears are pricked and alert. Her soft, black coat is dry and a delight to touch. She is already used to humans and enjoys being petted.

Introduction

DONKEYS were among the first animals to be domesticated; their capacity for carrying heavy loads, their surefootedness and their modest demand for food have been valued for many centuries and in surprisingly diverse parts of the world.

The domesticated donkey originated in North Africa and is superbly adapted to flourish in arid, stony, desert conditions. There, food was sparse; donkeys had to manage with low-nutrition plants and travel long distances over rocky terrain to gather them. Their small, oval, concave hooves gave them a firm, sure grip. They grazed in small groups, and in order to keep in touch with the other groups they developed loud voices and large ears which picked up the most distant calls of their fellow donkeys. They were able to survive quite long periods with very little water.

Although his qualities of surefootedness and endurance are still appreciated, it is the temperament of the donkey that has helped to revive his popularity. Unlike a horse, which often panics when confronted with a frightening situation and runs blindly into fences and other trouble, the donkey has a calmer, more stoical nature, and finds it less effort to stand still than to run away. For the inexperienced equine-fancier, the donkey's readiness to endure and forgive has much appeal — a donkey seems more manageable than a horse.

The donkey is very intelligent, and his ability to think of ways of avoiding doing the things he does not wish to has given rise to his reputation for stubbornness. However, a well-trained donkey is capable of a lot of hard, uncomplaining work.

His basic trust and liking for humans make him a delightful friend and his sense of fun is a joy to all those who have had the good fortune to know him.

All donkey owners appreciate the privilege of observing the daily routine and social life of their charges. Donkey watching is indeed an absorbing pastime.

Every young animal is delightful, but perhaps the baby donkey is one of the most captivating. Mother donkey is very attentive and never far away from her baby, ready to supply him with sustenance, security, advice and even discipline when required.

The donkey's gestation period (the time when the baby donkey grows in the mother's womb) is about 12 months. This is a month longer than the gestation period of a horse. Foaling is usually quick and easy, so that it is quite possible to miss seeing this event, even if you are keeping a close

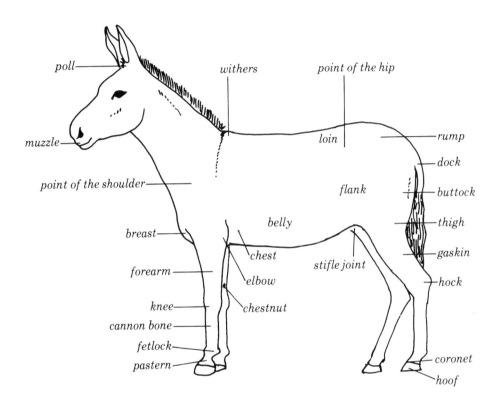

poll

withers

point of the hip

muzzle

loin

rump

dock

point of the shoulder

flank

buttock

thigh

belly

breast

chest

gaskin

stifle joint

forearm

elbow

hock

knee

chestnut

cannon bone

fetlock

coronet

pastern

hoof

PARTS OF THE DONKEY

watch as the time draws near.

The foal is on his feet within a few minutes of his arrival and his mother skilfully encourages his clumsy efforts at walking and guides him with her nose to her milk bag.

Donkeys are very sociable and

Pilar is a picture of contented motherhood as her foal, Yoyo, takes his evening drink.

form firm friendships. They can become very upset if separated from their companions. Mother donkey is very jealous of her foal for the first few weeks — rightly so, for the others are always on the lookout for a chance to steal its affections. Once the foal has firmly established who its mother is, it is allowed to play with the other foals, and a young jenny (mare) may be permitted to play the role of "aunty".

A pecking order is formed. The "boss" donkey has first turn at the food bin and the rolling patch and keeps the others in order with threatening looks and the occasional kick. Donkeys rarely hurt each other. A donkey that means "business" will strike with its forelegs rather than kick with its hind.

Rolling is an important ritual, done with enthusiasm and sensuous enjoyment. Your donkeys will make bare patches in your paddocks so that they can roll in the dust. A dusty coat is a comfortable coat for donkeys. They particularly appreciate freshly burnt areas, but be sure the

In the cool of the evening the foals start to frisk and play. Aloha is galloping as fast as she can — for the sheer exhilaration of it.

"Boss" donkey, Pilar, with ears laid back and tail swishing, warns Esmeralda to keep her distance from the coveted food bin.

"What bliss!" Yoyo indulges in a wonderful, dusty bath.

embers are cold before allowing the donkeys near — they have been known to roll in the hot ashes!

Donkeys sleep more often, but for shorter periods, than we do. They can sleep quite well standing up, as the muscles and ligaments in their legs lock so that the donkeys can relax and rest without falling over. Young donkeys usually lie down to sleep, however.

Coat care is given much

Nana wakes from an early morning snooze. She has been dozing on her feet to be ready to protect her foal. Violetta's role of "aunty" is less demanding, so she could lie down to sleep with the new arrival.

attention. There are few parts of its body that a donkey cannot reach with his teeth or hind hooves. For those places he seeks out a convenient tree or stump to rub against. It is therefore very important that the donkey is not wearing a halter when loose in the paddock. There are horrifying stories of donkeys that have broken their necks because their halters have become tangled.

Mutual grooming is a sign of friendship and trust between two donkeys. They gently bite around the neck and withers of their friends, an area which is difficult for donkeys to reach satisfactorily by themselves. They derive much pleasure from this.

Pilar rather inelegantly fixes a ticklish spot.

Pilar nibbles gently at her foal's neck and Yoyo learns to reciprocate.

Keeping Your Donkey

BEFORE you consider buying a donkey, you should be sure that you can supply him with his basic needs. These are: a paddock, food, water, shelter, a small amount of care and lots of time.

A PADDOCK

Your donkey will need a paddock of at least half a hectare (about one acre) — more if the vegetation is sparse or you don't want to give him much extra feed. Never give him less as he needs plenty of room to exercise, particularly when young.

The type of fence you construct for your donkey should be care-fully considered. The safest and by far the most expensive is a wooden post and rails, but it is not practicable for larger paddocks.

If your donkeys are sharing with cattle, barbed wire will be needed to contain the cattle. The top wire should, however, be plain and the bottom one low enough to discourage your donkey from crawling under it. The wires must be well supported and tensioned — slack fences are very dangerous.

If you are fencing only donkeys, mesh wire is excellent, providing that they cannot get their heads through the wire.

Electric fences are very effec-tive and take all the hassle out of controlling your jack (stallion).

A POST AND RAIL STYLE FENCE

FOOD

Donkeys eat a wider range of plants than horses and they need a diet of more roughage and less protein. They browse, rather like goats, and enjoy some unlikely delicacies, such as mandarin peels and peppermints. They thrive on our native grasses, which are preferable to soft introduced grasses, some of which can result in calcium deficiency if they are all that is available to the donkey.

During the winter or a dry period, it may be necessary to supplement their food. Good quality hay should be enough, but for working donkeys, lactating jennies or weaners, a small amount of some higher protein food might be needed. Pony pellets are useful for this as they provide balanced nutrition and are easy to handle.

Do not allow your donkey to become too fat. A serious problem called "foundering" can result

Esmeralda is separated from her friends and anxiously seeks to find a way back to them — but she respects the fence. This fence, made of three strands of barbed wire and a plain wire top strand, is designed for cattle but works well for most donkeys, too. It would be unsatisfactory, however, for containing a jack (stallion).

If you have several donkeys, a hay rack is ideal.

If you use a hay net be sure to fasten it up high as it drops down when empty. Donkeys sometimes paw when they are feeding and it is easy for them to get a foot caught in the net.

which causes the donkey great distress and can permanently deform his feet. Some donkeys develop a taste for the bark of your favourite trees, but this can easily be fixed with a coat of creosote — to the tree, not the donkey!

Always feed your donkey off the ground so as not to encourage the spread of worms. If you have several donkeys, a hay rack is ideal. The tray prevents the nutritious leafy part of the hay from being wasted on the ground.

Donkeys need a good supply of clean water.

WATER

A copious supply of clean water is essential. The trough should be regularly scrubbed and any algae or dead leaves removed.

Your donkeys will also appreciate and benefit from a mineral lick. Make sure that you have one that is safe for equines; some of the cattle licks contain urea and are poisonous to donkeys.

SHELTER

In warm and temperate climates a shed is not essential as long as the donkey has shelter from the sun, the wind and the rain. A thick hedge or fence, to protect him from the prevailing wind, and a nice shady tree are usually sufficient. However, nothing looks more miserable than a donkey in the rain, with his ears flattened

Iota escorts her newborn foal, Sir Thomas Tom, from the stable where he was born to meet the world outside.

and his tail tucked in! He is trying to convince you that he is a member of an ill-used and down-trodden race, born to suffer. So *you* will feel much better if you provide a shed for him, even if he disdains to use it.

A shed will certainly be appreciated if the flies are bad, and shelter is essential if your jenny is going to foal. A baby donkey's fluffy coat looks very warm but it is not waterproof, so foals should be kept dry for the first few weeks of their lives.

Make sure that your jenny is familiar with your stable *before* she foals. A jenny that is worried by being confined does not make a good mother.

Pilar looks pathetically unhappy in the rain.

Nana and Aloha enjoy the shelter of a bauhinia tree.

A SMALL AMOUNT OF CARE

Donkeys are very hardy and their health rarely gives cause for concern. They are, by nature, very placid and so do not panic and bolt like the more excitable horse, making them less prone to cuts and bumps. There are two areas, however, where care is always needed — donkeys' *parasites* and *feet*.

All donkeys have worms which need to be kept in check if the donkey is to be happy and healthy. If the worms are not controlled their numbers become enormous and they cause serious damage to the donkey's organs

Nana receives her dose of worming paste and Hadji, the dog, supervises carefully to make sure that she receives the correct dose. The donkey's mouth should be empty before drenching, otherwise he cleverly manages to spit the paste out, usually over you!

A freshly rasped hoof clearly shows the outside wall of the foot separated from the sole by the white line, and the triangular frog.

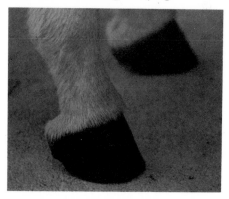

Violetta's front hooves are in good condition — short, level and free from chips and cracks. The front of the hoof should slope at the same angle as the pastern.

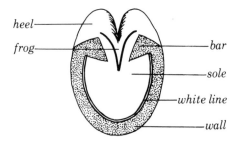

UNDERSIDE OF A DONKEY'S HOOF

and arteries as the migrating larvae burrow into the tissues. A wormy donkey will be thin, with a rough coat, and will probably rub his tail. He will look poor and feel worse. Bad infections of worms can cause colic and even death.

The best way to keep their numbers under control is by good husbandry and hygiene. The worms spread by laying eggs which are passed out in the donkey's dung. If the donkey is forced to eat close to this dung, he will be reinfected. Donkeys kept in small enclosures where the grass is sour and damp are likely to carry a high burden of worms. The young, the old and the weak are particularly likely to suffer.

It helps if you collect the donkeys' droppings, and their paddock should be divided into at least two parts so that each in turn can be spelled. The worm eggs are most susceptible to hot, dry weather so resting your paddock at such a time would be most beneficial.

Modern worming pastes come in tubes with a plunger, making it quite easy to squeeze the required dose on to the back of the donkey's tongue. Donkeys which are kept in conditions favouring the spread of worms should be dosed every six weeks, to keep them looking and feeling well.

Donkeys originated in the desert and their feet have adapted to the hard conditions of dry, stony ground. When we bring them to moist, soft, coastal pastures their feet grow faster than they are worn down, so it is necessary to correct this by regular rasping. Their feet should be kept short, neat and level.

Regular hoofcare is a *must* and is not difficult. If you cannot see yourself doing it every six weeks or so or having it done by a farrier, then don't buy a donkey.

In order to care for your donkey's feet you will need: a hoofpick (a blunt screwdriver does as well); a rasp — the Surform rasp with interchangeable blades is ideal; and a glove for your left hand (or right, if you are left-handed). Donkeys rarely need to be shod.

If neglected, a donkey's feet will grow out of shape, curling up at the toe and under at the sides. This will force their owner to walk on his heels. As well as causing endless agony, misshapen feet will throw unnatural stress on to the tendons at the back of the leg and permanent deformity can easily result.

Immense cruelty is inflicted on so many donkeys by neglect of their feet.

Even well-cared-for feet can occasionally suffer from seedy-toe, an infection of the white line of the hoof, to which donkeys are particularly prone. It again results from keeping donkeys on moist, soft grass. It can be controlled by digging out the infected area and packing the hole with cotton wool soaked in a fungicide. A ten percent formalin solution or a strong copper sulphate solution is effective. If it is neglected, seedy-toe can sometimes cause serious deformities of the hoof.

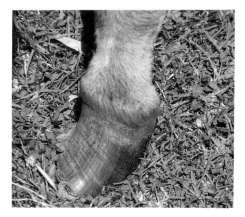

The owner of this foot, Flicka, was suffering from neglect. Her twisted hoof was already causing her to walk unevenly. Fortunately, it was not too late to fix the problem but at least six months of regular trimming will be required before the foot is back to normal.

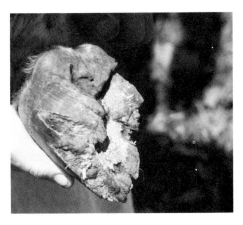

It is depressing to come across donkeys with obviously deformed feet. Their owners seem to be unaware of the suffering their ignorance or neglect can cause.

A Surform rasp for your donkey's footcare.

Training Your Donkey

DONKEYS may appear to be cuddly pets — and indeed they are — but they are not animated teddy bears. They do not automatically understand what their owners want, nor does it automatically occur to them to obey if they do understand.

They have to be trained so they can be enjoyed to the full and be useful.

The first step is to catch your donkey. A confident, trusting donkey will come when called, accept a titbit politely, and stand quietly while you put on his halter.

Not all donkeys are this well-behaved, although they all could become so given time, patience and that great attraction, food. Firstly, lure your donkey into a small enclosure or a yard so that you can get him into a corner. An inexperienced or nervous donkey may present you with his rump — but if his back is hunched and his tail tucked in, don't worry, he is not thinking of kicking. Rub him on both sides and keep talking, gradually working your way to his shoulder. Your aim is to get the donkey to relax while you are standing close by his shoulder with your arm around his neck. Never grab at the donkey, especially his head. Keep your hands low and move slowly.

When the donkey is accustomed to your closeness, you can quietly slip a rope around his neck and put on the halter.

Donkeys rarely kick but flattened ears and a swishing tail are signs of their displeasure. This should be quickly countered with a few sharp words and a smack with anything handy. A well-aimed kick from you will work wonders, too, for it is of vital importance that the donkey looks upon you as "boss" in the pecking order, right from the start.

Titbits are an excellent means of persuading your donkey to come when you want him. But, be careful, some owners seem unable to resist the urge to win their donkey's affection with food. These donkeys become very demanding and pushy, not waiting to differentiate between fingers and carrots when they snatch. You must gain your donkey's respect before indulging yourself in indulging him. Reserve these presents for a first greeting or a very special reward.

The object of tie-up lessons is to let your donkey discover that, however hard he struggles and pulls and however much he fidgets, he cannot escape. It is much less trouble to stand quietly. It is, therefore, most important that the halter and rope are strong and their buckles and clips cannot come undone. It

You can start training your donkey very early in his life. His first lesson should be to learn to accept humans and enjoy their company.

The donkeys follow Shona around the paddock as if she were the Pied Piper. They are seeking attention as well as hoping for a present.

Donkeys can be taught to accept presents carefully with their lips. Any signs of demanding or snatching must immediately be corrected.

is surprising how powerful even the smallest foal can be. If your gear breaks, it is not only expensive, but your donkey will have learned the wrong lesson. Make sure that whatever object you tie your donkey to is safe and secure. There should be no sharp edges or places where he can get a foot caught.

Tie the rope about level with his head and quite short so that he

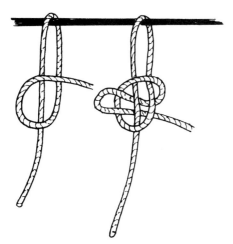

Use a quick-release knot for tying up your donkey.

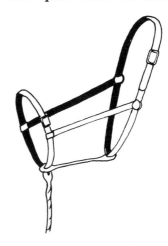

When tying up your donkey, the rope should be attached to the noseband of his halter.

Use a sack to tie up a very strong donkey.

When he is used to the feel of the halter, accustom your donkey to being tied up. Having his head and freedom restricted are quite hard for him to accept, so he will pull back and struggle for a while.

cannot get it wrapped around his neck. Use a quick-release knot and never go away and leave him struggling.

For a very strong donkey it is a good idea to attach the rope to a wide strap or a folded bag around his neck. This distributes the pull and is more comfortable. The rope should pass through the nose band of his halter.

Try to get him to stand up and relax by talking to him and rubbing him under his tail. Do not release him until he is quiet. The first lesson should be short; as he gets used to it, you can increase the time he spends tied up.

Donkeys love being groomed. As well as making them look smart, grooming is an opportunity to check them for ticks, lice, scratches and other problems. It is particularly appreciated when the donkey is shedding his winter coat.

A soft-bristled body brush for short coats and sensitive areas.

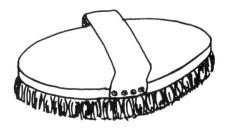

A stiff-bristled dandy brush for winter coats.

A rubber curry comb to clean your brushes — and mud from your donkey.

A long-handled comb — a great help when the winter coat is being shed.

Your donkey, however, does not feel that his coat is in really good condition unless it is full of dust, so don't be surprised if, after all your hard work, your clean and shiny donkey avails himself of the first opportunity to roll!

As well as allowing himself to be groomed and handled all over, your donkey must, most importantly, let you pick up, clean out and rasp his feet.

To pick up a donkey's front or hind hoof you should face the opposite way to the donkey and stand close to him. Run your hand down his leg, so that he knows what you are going to do. When you reach the fetlock, the joint above the hoof, gently squeeze and ask the donkey to pick up his foot. Old hands will have already adjusted their weight and raised

their foot — but the less experienced may need more persuasion. Never grip the foot as this will cause the donkey to resist and maybe kick.

Having raised the foot do not allow him to put it down until you permit it. Put the foot down gently — don't just drop it. Hind legs can become a bit excited sometimes. If the donkey kicks, relax and follow the movement; he will tire before you do, especially if you are not standing too far back.

When teaching your donkey to lead, remember that pulling will get you nowhere. The accelerator is at the back and is activated by a tap from the whip or by tweaking some hair in the sensitive flank area.

Stand by the donkey's left

"You're tickling."   *"That's better."*

shoulder facing the same way as the donkey. Hold his lead rope in your left hand and your whip over his back in your right. Tell the donkey to walk forwards. Make up your mind from the outset how you are going to communicate with your donkey. You may either click your tongue or say "walk on" or "forwards" — you must then stick to that command. If you decide to click your tongue be careful not to overdo it, for if you keep on clicking, the donkey will cease to notice it.

If your donkey does not respond to your word command, tap him increasingly firmly with the whip until he does. As soon as he shows *any* inclination to obey, stop tapping and praise him. Keep

your position by his shoulder all the time, even if it means a few fancy steps on your part. Use the whip to help him keep straight and don't allow him to lean on you. Use a word of command as well as a tug on the halter when you want him to stop.

It is more conventional to hold the donkey's lead in your right hand and tap behind you with the whip in your left. I find it all too easy to tap my own legs instead of the donkey and, being right-handed, have more control with the whip in my right hand. When the donkey is going forwards it is then possible to steady him with your right hand on his neck — just as his mother did with her chin when he was a foal. It is very

Shona shows Naomi how to pick up and clean out Pilar's front hoof.

Naomi manages to pick out the back hoof by herself.

useful to be able to steer your donkey like this when you don't have a halter handy and it is a pleasant feeling to go for a walk with an arm around a donkey's neck!

Take him for lots of walks and gradually introduce as many new situations as you can think of — cars, people, dogs.

Donkeys usually dislike dogs. They will quickly get to know your own dog and even accept him as a friend, but always keep an eye open for folks who come visiting with their beloved pooch. These dogs are unaware that donkeys mean trouble. They may not be as young and agile as they used to be and so are unable to escape from the donkey's well-aimed strikes and kicks.

Friendships can be strained by donkeys attacking dogs but this natural instinct is handy if dingoes are around.

Your donkey must learn to accept all manner of strange flapping objects. He must not be alarmed if you appear one windy day in a billowing skirt, or on a wet one in a bright, crackly raincoat with an umbrella. He must not flinch if flapped in the face by the branch of a tree, or if you want to festoon him in a bright saddle cloth or some strange manner of fancy dress. He must learn not to be perturbed by any of the extraordinary things that people have and do.

This lesson is known as "bagging" and in its simplest form consists of flicking your donkey all over with a sack until you are both bored to tears and he does not even notice the flicking any more. Flick and rub his flanks, belly, shoulder and head; tie the sack to a rope and weave it in and out of his legs along the ground. Repeat with a different type of sack, a raincoat, an umbrella, and any other object, until you are sure that there is nothing that exists that can scare your donkey.

Food and friends can save a lot of hassle as we can see in the pictures on the following pages.

A whip suitable for a donkey.

Pulling will get you nowhere.

With Shona by her shoulder, donkey Fifi walks along cheerfully.

Hadji, the dog, would like to play but Fifi's instinct tells her that it would be unwise. Hadji had to be protected from the donkeys when he was a puppy but soon learned to keep out of their paddock. He has supreme confidence that he is safe with any donkey that has a halter or bridle on and is attached to a human. His main complaint is that when children come visiting he is upstaged by the donkeys!

Violetta was nervous of sacks, especially the noisy, crackly kind. She was festooned with them and left in a safe yard to work the problem out for herself.

Aloha is introduced to an umbrella and a sack dragging along the ground. At first she looked appalled but soon they ceased to worry her.

Conchita is very suspicious of the wheelbarrow.

Esmeralda has more experience of the world and is always hopeful that food might be around!

In order not to miss out, Conchita overcomes her fears and joins in the feast.

Once the donkey develops confidence in his handler, he will accept new and spooky situations calmly. In these pictures, a donkey learns that walking through water isn't so awful after all.

"No, I won't — it's obviously not safe," the donkey appears to be thinking as he is coaxed towards the water.

"Smells O.K. — but it's wet!" The donkey still rejects the unfamiliar.

"Well, if you'll come with me and we keep to the shallow bit," he thinks as he finally agrees to a little wading.

It is a great help if you teach your donkey to obey word commands — walk, trot, halt and back. You can teach these when you are going on your walks, but your donkey should also obey you from a distance while working in a round yard or on a lunging rein.

A long lunging whip is necessary to keep your donkey walking and trotting around you in a circle. Do not try to teach all the commands at once — your donkey will be confused. Keep these lessons very short as most donkeys cannot see the point of running around in circles and quickly get bored. You could find yourself doing all the work.

Don't forget to change direction and to teach your donkey to stand still and square when he halts.

The next step is to teach your donkey to long-rein. To start with, use a snug-fitting halter made of soft material or, better still, a drop noseband which is padded across the nose. You will need a surcingle with rings placed low so as to keep the long-reins down. Work in an enclosed area at first, as you always should when introducing your donkey to a new idea.

Gradually drop back from your leading position until your donkey is walking in front of you. Try to keep in position behind him — he will find it a bit strange — so don't forget to reassure him and praise him when he obeys.

Do lots of turns along the fence and use the same word commands you used when leading him until he associates them with pressure from the reins. Be gentle but firm.

If he decides to ignore your request to turn, don't pretend that you didn't ask, insist on obedience, even if it takes a while to get it. Try to keep him always going forwards, for then he has no choice but to obey. You are teaching your donkey to respond to a feeling, not physically trying to turn or stop him, so your voice commands are very important.

When he is calm and obedient you can go on your familiar walks with your donkey driven in front of you. Strive for a response to the very lightest touch on the reins.

When, and only when, he is leading freely, obeying your voice and long-reining smoothly in a halter, your donkey can be introduced to a bridle.

The donkey's bridle needs to have a longer browband than that for a horse, to accommodate all those brains and those beautiful ears. Your saddler will make one for you; if not, get another saddler. The bridle must be

A long lunging whip is necessary to keep your donkey walking and trotting around you in a circle.

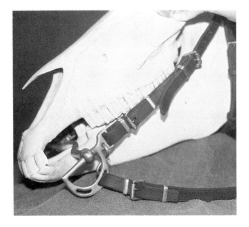

The bit rests in the gap between the donkey's incisors and his numerous huge molars. It is normally cushioned from the sensitive bony jaw by the tongue. This bit is a port-mouthed Spanish snaffle. It can exert a slight leverage effect if the reins are attached lower and a curb chain used. This is rarely necessary for a donkey.

comfortable — so must the bit.

The bit sits in the gap between the donkey's incisors and his huge grinding molars. It is normally cushioned from the sensitive bony jaw by the tongue. However, some donkeys are adept at getting their tongues over the bit, making things uncomfortable for both of you.

A donkey cannot eat with his tongue over the bit so, when you first put the bit in his mouth, offer some food to encourage him to keep it in the correct position. It may help to keep the donkey's mouth closed with a drop nose-band, but don't let him eat with it buckled up as he could easily choke.

There is a wide and confusing range of bits at your saddlers to choose from and everyone has his or her personal favourite. My preference for a donkey is an unjointed bit, like the Spanish snaffle, as it does not drop down in the mouth like a jointed one. I dislike bits with cheek bars as they can catch in fences and saddles with very unfortunate results. They do help to stop the bit from pulling through the mouth should the donkey resist the pressure of the bit, but a drop noseband will do the same job by keeping the mouth closed.

Do not rush these early stages for they form the foundation of your donkey's education. In order to be a welcome and useful member of society, he needs to know all about donkey manners.

The donkey's bridle needs to have a longer browband than that for a horse.

Work on a lunging rein helps to make donkeys obedient to word commands. As they soon become bored with repetitious circles, introduce a little jump to enliven the procedure.

Long-reining teaches your donkey to obey pressure from the reins. It is a very important stage in his education and lays the foundation for him to be the proud possessor of a "good mouth".

Don't forget to teach your donkey to back — some find it quite hard to believe that reversing is possible.

A trot will do you both a world of good!

You can start to train your donkey when he is quite young. Keep his lessons short as he cannot concentrate for long and needs to tell mum about his adventures!

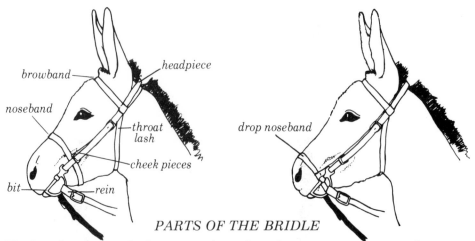

PARTS OF THE BRIDLE

The browband *must be long enough so that the ears are not cramped.*

The throat lash *should allow four fingers clearance — it will tighten as the donkey raises his head.*

The cheek pieces *should be adjusted so that the bit just creases the corners of the lips, giving the donkey a suspicion of a smile.*

The noseband *is only ornamental and should have room for two fingers between it and the donkey's nose. They are best avoided on donkeys under four years of age who are still teething.*

The drop noseband *may be used instead of the ordinary noseband. It is fitted below the bit and helps to keep the donkey's mouth closed. Do not let him eat while it is done up or he may choke.*

He must stand still when required and lead freely, not pulling, pushing or dragging behind. He must turn willingly — a head and neck braced against you, or a head that turns without its body following it around, are just not acceptable. Pushing you with his head or leaning and, in particular, barging in gateways, are punishable offences. He should turn around and wait politely while you fasten the latch.

Leaving his friends, even temporarily, is difficult for the donkey to agree to and he will probably make a fuss and a lot of noise. Never give in to him — it may be necessary to enforce your demand with a tap from the whip.

Make quite sure that he understands what you are asking and then be firm. A donkey is very intelligent, only too aware of any weakness in his owner's resolve, and very ready to exploit it.

Think of lots of ways to vary lessons, for donkeys are easily bored. Never handle your donkey if you are short of time or temper. Don't be tempted to try something new at the end of a lesson. Be prepared to cut things short if you are especially pleased with his progress or you find your patience wearing thin. Always end on a high note and if necessary go back and repeat something you know he can do before quitting. Once you have both mastered these early essentials, the rest is easy.

Being Useful

THERE are many ways in which your donkey can help around your property. They seem to be natural "pullers" and this instinct can be put to good use by getting them to move all sorts of heavy, awkward objects.

Previously tedious, difficult jobs become fun when a donkey is around to help.

Snigging is the term used for pulling something along the ground. For light work a padded breastplate is adequate, fitted so that it doesn't interfere with the donkey's windpipe or inhibit his shoulder movement. From the breastplate come the traces which are held up by a loin strap so that they are less likely to tangle with the donkey's hind legs.

For the same reason a swingle bar is used to hold the traces apart.

Introduce your donkey to snigging by dragging something along the ground behind him as you go for a walk. A sack stuffed with straw is easy to pull, but make sure it is on a bumpy surface and makes lots of noise. When your donkey is quite happy about this, it is safe to attach it to the swingle bar and the donkey. Stay by your donkey's head until he is used to being followed by that awful "thing", but then drive him from behind, as it is easier to control the "thing" from there.

Here the donkeys "earn their keep" hauling a load of firewood.

This swingle bar is a piece of pipe with a chain threaded through it. The chain is attached to the traces with quick-release clips. A swivel welded to the centre of the swingle bar is essential.

For "serious" work, like harrowing, it is best to use a collar as it distributes the load evenly over the donkey's shoulders and gives him more pulling power.

The donkey's strength and patience can be put to good use around a farm. Here Siegi is harrowing the new strawberry patch.

Rather than carrying heavy, prickly bales of hay to your donkeys, let them do the work! This bale is being towed along on a sack. It is easier for the donkey to pull, and for you to manoeuvre the load, if you keep the traces short.

Snigging harness is quite simple and easy to make. Esmeralda's is made from nylon webbing.

The travois is an American Indian invention and is ideal for light loads. It is cheap and simple to make from bamboo poles, hessian and binder twine. Cross struts are needed to keep the two poles apart. It is attached to a saddle pad. A simple breastplate is needed to keep the pad from slipping back. Use it to carry hedge clippings to the compost heap or, as here, to collect grass mowings to mulch your garden.

It helps if you train your donkey to stand unattended — this is not usually very difficult as, sensibly enough, they find it less trouble to stay put than to move. It might occur to them, however, to wander off in search of food or friends.

If your donkey is nervous, try blinkers to prevent him from seeing what is following. Most don't need them but, for those that do, they make all the difference. Some donkeys, however, are made more nervous by not being able to see behind them. Your donkey will let you know.

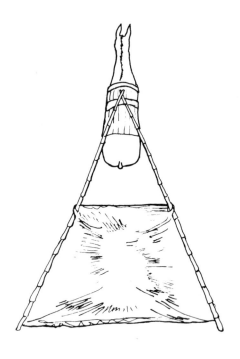

THE TRAVOIS

A donkey pulling a travois is ideal for light loads.

Going on a picnic? The donkey provides transport for the feast.

The donkey's strength and patience can be put to good use around a farm. For this more "serious" work it is best to use a collar, as it distributes the load evenly over the donkey's shoulders and gives him more pulling power. The collar must fit snugly to avoid chafe.

A sledge is very versatile and can be used to carry firewood, hay, manure and even you!

It is quite a challenge to match a pair; not only should they be comparable in size and colour, but, more importantly, they should both be equally as prepared to work.

As well as pulling things along the ground, the donkey can help you by carrying a pack on his back.

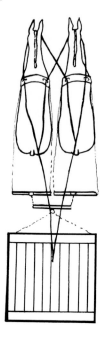

A sledge is very versatile when used for pulling loads.

Here Philippa, the donkey, makes herself useful in the orange orchard. The panniers are attached to a pack saddle and must be kept evenly balanced.

It is quite a challenge to match a pair. They should be comparable in size and colour and both equally as prepared to work!

If you enjoy bushwalking but don't want to carry all the provisions on your back, a donkey is the answer.

Donkeys and Children

DONKEYS and children go together naturally. Donkeys are ideal first mounts and quite young children can learn the basics of caring for their pet and riding him. Most donkeys enjoy the attention of their young charges and will show great patience and sympathy.

Safety first is the rule. Adequate footwear is a must, just in case the donkey accidentally treads on an unprotected toe. The child should not be allowed to feed him titbits, except with supervision. Even the most careful donkey can mistake a small finger for a goodie.

Children should be taught to be quiet and calm and on no account to run up to a donkey. A donkey rarely kicks but a sudden noisy approach from behind, where he cannot see, can upset even the most reliable pet. He needs to know where you are and what you are going to do.

The child can saddle the donkey but an adult should always check that it is secure and the girth is firm. Clog stirrups ensure that small feet cannot slip right through and a crupper is essential to prevent the saddle from sliding forwards.

The child should mount from the near side while the helper holds the donkey and supports the saddle from the off side.

Adjust the stirrups and check the girth again. Keep a hold on the donkey's leading rein.

The child should hold on to the saddle, not the helper, otherwise he or she will never get good balance. If necessary, place a hand on the rider's knee to encourage him to keep it on the saddle. For the very nervous, a second helper can assist from the other side.

Donkeys and children are an ideal combination.

Most donkeys enjoy the attention of children and will show great patience and sympathy.

Putting on a bridle presents quite a challenge.

Opposite: *Naomi and Pilar, the donkey, share a confidence. Donkeys are particularly responsive to children and often tolerate them more than they would an adult. Pilar is very safe and can be totally relied upon to care for any children entrusted to her.*

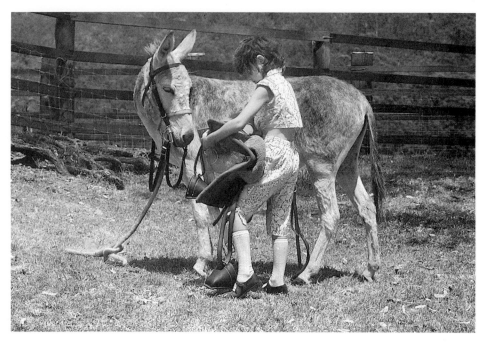

Pilar, the donkey, advises Naomi on the problems of putting on her saddle. A child can saddle the donkey but an adult should always check that it is secure and the girth is firm.

Clog stirrups ensure that small feet cannot slip right through, and a crupper is essential to prevent the saddle from sliding forwards.

When mounting the donkey, the child should hold on to the saddle, not the helper, so that he or she will learn good balance. Mounting is always from the donkey's left side.

When teaching a child to ride, keep the donkey on a leading rein and walk him in a circle around you.

The object of these early lessons is to give the child confidence and accustom him to the correct position in the saddle.

Keep the donkey on the leading rein and walk him in a circle around you. Talk to the child and the donkey and try to get everyone to relax and feel happy.

Don't try to do too much — Rome wasn't built in a day! The child will be using new muscles and will tire quickly.

Eventually the exciting moment comes when the child is so confident, and the donkey so well-trained, that they can go it alone.

Until the child is a strong enough rider to be in complete control of the donkey, rides should be supervised by an adult, or be in the company of other donkeys. Donkeys very quickly find out if their rider cannot quite manage them and readily take advantage of it.

Opposite and above: *Exercises are invaluable to strengthen the child's balance and seat.*

Eventually the exciting moment comes when the child is so confident, and the donkey so well-trained, that they can go it alone.

Riding and Driving Your Donkey

WHEN a donkey is three years old, he can be lightly ridden.

Before this age, although he may look strong, the cartilage in his knee joints is too soft to carry heavy weights for long periods. At four, he is ready for plenty of work.

A donkey rarely worries when first introduced to a saddle and a rider. He should be started in an enclosed area and, if possible, have an older, steady donkey to accompany him on his first few outings.

The donkey's back is straighter than that of a horse, with a less pronounced wither and flatter ribs. However, most saddles will fit him, provided that a crupper can be attached to stop the saddle from slipping forwards. Pad saddles are satisfactory for lightweight riders but, having no tree, they do not keep the weight off the donkey's backbone and should not be used by adults.

Larger donkeys make excellent mounts for adults so, if your children are hooked on donkeys, you can join in the fun and go riding with them, even if you are doubtful that your riding ability is up to managing a more spirited horse.

The well-trained donkey will remember his manners and walk calmly and willingly, even if you don't have the time to ride him regularly. He is, therefore, ideal for older folk and busy mums and dads.

His comfortable gaits adapt easily to your ability, or your mood. He is quite happy at a sedate walk while you admire the countryside; for the more adventurous, he is capable of a brisk walk, a smart trot, and a very comfortable canter. Donkeys jump well, and on steep, difficult terrain they come into their own for they are very sure-footed.

Donkeys are very alert to what is under their feet and often object to a change of surface. Concrete, long grass, water, wooden bridges, bitumen roads, especially those with white lines, are particularly troublesome.

Introduce him to these hazards at home where you have plenty of time to persuade him to walk over them, rather than wait until you are on the trail ride.

The more your donkey is used to strange and varied surfaces, the less he will object when he meets a new one.

Also, cattle work isn't only for stock horses — donkeys can do an excellent job. At first they may be a little nervous of the large beasts and your loud shouts and your waving, but soon they become used to it and enjoy all the excitement.

The saddle should be comfortable for both the donkey and the rider. The Military saddle (above) and the Western saddle (below) are both ideal for donkeys.

Donkeys are fun to ride — for children and mums and dads!

Donkeys are very strong for their size, so if some members of the family are not confident of controlling their mounts, doubling up is the answer.

Driving a donkey is one of the delights of this life; wandering through the forest or trotting along the byways in a donkey cart is an experience that too many donkey owners miss.

It is a small step in donkey training from pulling a sledge to pulling a cart. If they are obedient and untroubled by being followed by a sledge, they are unlikely to find anything to perturb them about a cart. They quite readily accept the shafts, the weight on their backs and the noise of the cart following them.

For the owner, putting the donkey into harness is a bigger step. Carts and harness can be (but need not be) rather expensive and, for those unused to driving, controlling the donkey from the cart seems more difficult than when riding him. When I first met traffic while driving a donkey, I wanted to jump into the ditch. The donkey trotted cheerfully on and put me to shame!

Do not be deterred, getting your donkey into harness is well worth the effort.

There is a long tradition attached to driving carts and to the harness that goes with them. If you are going to compete in the show ring, take note of this when choosing bit, noseband, blinkers, buckles, whip, colour of harness, and so on. For those who just want to go for a drive, anything goes, so long as it is strong, safe,

Edith refuses to cross a wooden bridge and it takes three people to persuade her to change her mind. She did eventually reach the other side!

Above: *Elise and Coco, the donkey, confidently descend a steep bank. Donkeys are sure-footed and agile, and are strong for their size, with powerful shoulders. They are capable of carrying their riders safely, even in the most difficult country.*

Right, top and bottom: *Coco is introduced to all sorts of hazards at home so that when he meets a strange situation out on the trail he will not be afraid of it.*

Cattle work isn't only for stock horses — donkeys can do an excellent job. They may be a little nervous of cattle at first but they soon get used to it and enjoy all the excitement.

They quickly learn to help you open and close gates.

Donkeys love jumping, too!

RIDING AND DRIVING YOUR DONKEY 63

and you and your donkey are happy.

Harness can be made of traditional leather, which has a feel all of its own, or of newer materials such as nylon webbing or plastic. They are all satisfactory provided that they are strongly made and a good fit.

The donkey pulls the cart from the traces which come from the collar or breastplate. The breeching passes around the donkey's buttocks and by leaning back into it he can brake the cart when going downhill. There is also a narrow saddle with a tree which takes the weight of the cart and supports the shafts.

Carts come with two or four wheels. Four-wheelers are more complicated as the front wheels

Camilla is harnessed to a low exercise cart. Home-made from pipe and plywood, it is cheap and comfortable. Her plain harness is made of leather and includes a breastplate.

must turn independently from the back for the cart to negotiate corners. They can carry larger loads and there is no weight on the donkey's back.

If you buy a two-wheeled cart, it is important to check its balance. Stand between the shafts and hold them up while somebody sits in the cart. Ask them to lean forward and to sit up straight. You will find that the weight on the shafts increases considerably when their weight is forwards. With a well-balanced cart the weight is negligible when the passengers are sitting up straight.

Check that the wheels are sturdy — bicycle wheels are not strong enough in most situations. The shafts should come to the point of the donkey's shoulder so that he can push against them when turning. The floor of the cart should be level and, of course, the donkey's hind legs should be clear of the front of the cart.

When driving your donkey it is essential to keep alert. You cannot feel what your donkey is thinking as you can when you are riding him. You have to watch his ears and tail, and the road ahead and behind, for signs that anything is worrying him. It is all too easy to be lulled into a daydream by the rhythmic trot and the passing scenery.

Keep a gentle feel on the reins and keep him going forwards, if necessary with a flick of your whip. Your donkey should not canter when pulling his cart. Try not to keep changing the pace as this is tiring for the donkey.

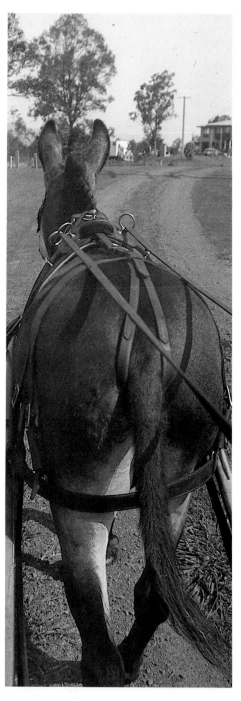

Going home! A view from the box seat — the donkey is trotting steadily and enjoying his outing.

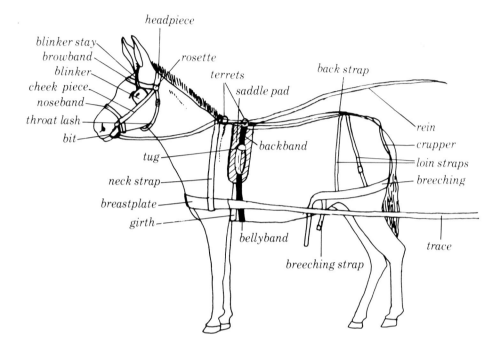

DRIVING HARNESS

The saddle pad *has a small tree which keeps the weight of the cart from the donkey's backbone. It is secured by the* girth *which does not have to be as tight as the one on a riding saddle.*

The backband *supports the* tugs *through which the shafts are passed. The flaps of the saddle pad prevent the tugs from rubbing the donkey's sides. The backband and tugs should be adjusted so that the floor of the cart is level. The* bellyband *is fastened loosely and prevents the shafts from rising.*

The breastplate *should be fitted so that it is not too low to allow free movement of the front legs, nor so high that it presses on the windpipe. It is held in place by the* neck strap. *From the breastplate come the* traces *which are attached to the cart. They should be sufficiently long so that there is no danger of the cart hitting the donkey's hind legs.*

The breeching *is used to brake the cart when going downhill. It is fitted into the curve of the buttocks so that the donkey can lean back into it. It is held in place by the* loin straps *which pass through the* backstrap.

The breeching strap *is wrapped around the shaft through a "D" fitting on the shaft.*

The driving bridle *is similar to a riding bridle except that it is often ornamented with rosettes and has* blinkers. *Special* bits *are available for driving, but the bit in which you ride your donkey is perfectly satisfactory.*

Donkeys love standing on a tub — it makes them feel important!

Just for Fun

DONKEYS gain much pleasure from standing on a tub — it makes them feel important. If left with one in their paddock they will spend quite long periods on it and even jostle each other for possession.

At first, you will have to show your donkey how to climb up, but he will soon get the hang of it. A jack will mount the tub with a neat rear.

You can lead your donkey from a horse — provided that the horse is a trusted friend and familiar with donkey antics. Be careful of your horse's mouth for, if the donkey pulls, it is all too easy to take the strain on your reins. Hold on to the saddle instead.

Invite your donkeys to tea occasionally . . . and into the house to see where you live and if there are any titbits around. They are usually clean but it doesn't hurt to have a bucket around in case of accidents. They will be attracted to, and probably not very good for, your latest flower arrangement!

Dressing up is even more fun when your donkey does it too!

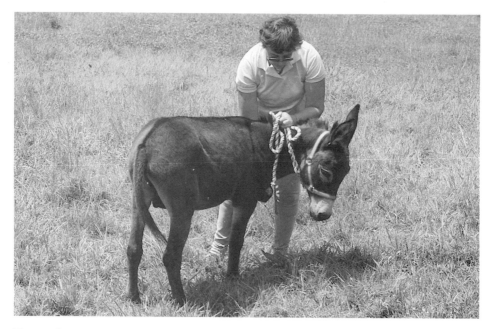

To teach your donkey to lie down, pick up his near-side foreleg and turn his head away to the off side. He will tire in this position and sink elegantly to the ground. Follow him down so that he will stay down until allowed to get up, even if it means a rather less dignified position on your part!

It is not difficult to teach your donkey to lie down to order, but be prepared for him to do it sometimes without being asked. Don't laugh when he makes a mistake; donkeys are very sensitive.

Invite your donkeys to tea occasionally . . .

This is a pyjam-ass!

A Word about Donkey Societies

MANY donkey societies exist in various parts of the world to help donkeys and their owners enjoy each other. They are concerned with the welfare of donkeys and very concerned with informing people about donkeys, their care, training and potential as useful animals as well as pets.

The societies serve to introduce donkey owners to each other so that they can discuss donkey matters, share problems, and enjoy their donkeys together. Field days, trail rides, gymkhanas, shows and fun days feature on the programme. Most societies keep a register of donkeys to encourage the breeding of good animals.

The Australian Donkey Breed Society is typical of these societies. In addition to organising activities for its members, the society sends out a monthly newsletter and has a high quality magazine, *Donkey Digest*, which is full of donkeys, donkey doings, and donkey ideas.

Donkey societies are for donkeys and people. They are concerned with informing people about their donkeys, their care, training and potential as useful animals as well as pets.

Field days are held regularly to give practical advice to donkey owners. All facets of donkey care, management and training are explained and members with donkey problems can bring them for discussion and advice.

Talks are held on harness, pasture management, gelding, foot care, bitting and all aspects of training. It's surprising what a diverse range of subjects can be related to donkeys! The Society is there to help.

Show time is an opportunity to show off your donkey and all the care and training you have put into him. Presentation is all-important — your donkey should be spotlessly clean and beautifully groomed. You will need to prepare well in advance to have him looking and behaving at his best for the big day. Don't forget to polish his hooves and to look smart yourself, too. The donkey is a proud and dignified animal so you should look neat and tidy to show him off.

Gymkhanas are less formal occasions and lots of fun. The donkeys really enjoy all the excitement and competing with each other. Quite often their particular sense of humour will disrupt the proceedings — but, hopefully, your own sense of fun will allow you to appreciate the situation all the more.

72　TO OWN A DONKEY

DONKEY SOCIETIES

UNITED STATES
American Donkey and
Mule Society,
Betsy Hutchins,
Rt 5 Box 65, Denton, Texas.

AUSTRALIA
Australian Donkey Breed Society,
Jenifer Simpson,
Booloumba Creek,
MS 16, Maleny, Qld 4552.

CANADA
Canadian Donkey and
Mule Association,
S. E. Sewell, Box 156
Leslieville, Alberta Tom 1 Ho.

DENMARK
Dansk Aesel Avl,
Lars Garden, Bomosevej 2,
DK — 4684 Holme-Olstrup.

UNITED KINGDOM
Donkey Breed Society,
Norman G. Price,
Duton Hill,
Dunmow, Essex.

NETHERLANDS
Dutch Donkey Breed Society,
Mevr A. Boeree-Rossberg,
Noorddijk 7,
1463 P J Noordbeemster.

SWEDEN
Svenska Asnefureningen,
Miss Catherina Asberg,
Sibyllegatan 31,
S-114 42 Stockholm.

NEW ZEALAND
New Zealand Donkey
Breed Society,
Barbara Vincent,
P. O. Box 109,
Manakau, Horowhenua.

The children's riding class at a donkey society gathering.

When a group of young enthusiasts sets off to go camping for the weekend, a pack donkey trots along behind with some of the gear.

A Donkey for You?

SO YOU have decided that you would like a donkey. Before you decide which donkey, go and see as many as you possibly can. There are many factors to take into consideration; donkeys are not all the same, any more than horses or dogs.

Firstly, there are jacks (stallions), jennies (mares) and geldings (de-sexed males).

A jenny is of course essential if, someday, you would like to breed a foal. But it is important to remember that you must accept the responsibility for the future welfare of the foal and you should not breed it unless you are sure that it will have a role to play in this world.

Jennies come in season every three weeks for about five days. This is the time they can become pregnant. They may be irritable and find it difficult to concentrate on your wishes, especially if there is a jack around. And jacks are always hopeful that their services might be needed. They proclaim their willingness with loud braying and boisterous showing off.

Jacks should always be gelded (de-sexed) unless they are very special and required for breeding.

The gelding is free of disadvantages and makes for an ideal pet or working donkey.

You may think a mature, well-trained and experienced donkey will best fill your need, or you may be tempted by a young one which can grow up with the family.

Donkeys are very sociable animals and will fret if they have no friend. They prefer another donkey but will form devoted relationships with horses, cattle and other animals. However, when you are buying a donkey, you should give serious thought to getting two.

Australian donkeys are mostly between 11 and 12 hands (one hand equals four inches — about ten centimetres — measured at the withers). A few are over 13 hands and the smaller ones are under ten hands. In Great Britain donkeys tend to be small but in the United States they come in a very wide range, from miniature (under nine hands) to mammoth donkeys, some of which reach 16 hands. These very large donkeys are used mainly for breeding mules.

Big donkeys are excellent for adults to ride and the little ones give confidence to the very young or nervous who may be overawed by a large animal. They all go well in harness.

They come in a wide range of colours, some with crosses and stripes, and some without. Some have shaggy coats, others quite short. There are elegant donkeys and donkeys that are beautiful only in the eyes of their owner.

Iota is in season. She shows the very typical "mouthing" and is looking around for a jack (stallion).

Coco is excited by the presence of a willing jenny (mare) and making a lot of noise.

Aaron and Yoyo introduce themselves.

However, they should all have the friendly, patient, unflappable donkey temperament.

Somewhere out there your donkey is waiting for you. Maybe one day you will wake up and find that the donkey in your dreams has become a reality...for wouldn't it be fun to be owned by a donkey?

Elizabeth snoozes with her hat on!
Picture: Patricia Goss.

Somewhere out there is a donkey who's just longing to meet...and own... you!

Index